MW00678053

Miracles!

Chronicled in One Man's Journey

Miracles!

Chronicled in One
Man's Journey

William Carr Blood

© Copyright 1995—William Carr Blood

All rights reserved. This book is protected under the copyright laws of the United States of America. This book may not be copied or reprinted for commercial gain or profit. The use of short quotations or occasional page copying for personal or group study is permitted and encouraged. Permission will be granted upon request. The Scripture quotations in this publication are from the New King James Version. Copyright © 1979, 1980, 1982, Thomas Nelson, Inc. Emphasis within Scripture quotes is the author's own.

Published by:

McDougal Publishing
P.O. Box 3595
Hagerstown, MD 21742
www.mcdougalpublishing.com

ISBN 1-58158-087-8
EAN 978-158158-087-7

Printed in the United States of America
For Worldwide Distribution

Library of Congress Catalog Card Number: 95-83204

Sixth Printing (Revised): 2005
Eighth Printing: 2009
Ninth Printing: 2012

Dedication

To

Leigh, Bert and Kasha,
our children,

and

Alice, Carroll, Mobley, Victoria,
Charles and Dana, their children,

and

Emma, Nathan, Joshua, Cooper, Gavyn
and Ella, their children's children.

"Write in a book for yourself all the words that
I have spoken to you" (Jeremiah 30:2).

"And teach them to your children and your
grandchildren" (Deuteronomy 4:9).

Memorial

George Henry Carr (1865-1950)

My mother's father told me about a miracle before
I was old enough to understand what a miracle was.
He was a teenage farmboy milking a cow in the family
barn near Clarence, New York, when God spoke to
him and told him to become a minister. My grandfather
was shocked at hearing this audible voice and quickly
got off his milking stool, knelt in the straw, and promised
to do what God asked. At age 33, he graduated from
Hamilton Theological Seminary of Colgate University
and became a dedicated pastor for as long as his
health permitted.

Whenever he told me about that day, I had an
awesome feeling about an invisible God speaking to
my grandfather and my grandfather's response to
what he heard. Later I realized my grandmother and
mother did not believe him because they did not think
God spoke to people. But I believed him! He was sincere
and consistent every time he told me, and his eyes

looked like he was back in the barn sitting on that small wooden stool, listening to the milk splash into the pail moments before hearing that marvelous voice.

"The memory of the righteous is blessed"
(Proverbs 10:7).

"The Lord...hears the prayer of the righteous"
(Proverbs 15:29).

"For this child I prayed..."
(1 Samuel 1:27).

"His children are blessed after him"
(Proverbs 20:7).

Appreciation

The English language is inadequate to express my appreciation for my wife's support in preparing this book. My lovely, tender and delicate Dottie is a perfectionist on the word processor. Her diligence often extended into late hours and she has a talent for editing which has reinforced my expressions.

Dorothy is truly a "gift from God," which is the meaning of her name.

Contents

Introduction

Everything in this book is true!

You will read about supernatural events that began in Hawaii and continued in North Carolina and Florida for eight years. The explosive reality of these incidents changed the direction of my life.

I am fully persuaded that the Source of these miracles knows everything about you and me and is interested in our thoughts, actions, and well-being every instant of our existence.

William Carr Blood

PART
1

Miracle Week

**"...you will be His witness to all men of what you
have seen and heard"**

(Acts 22:15)

CHAPTER
1

Hotel Room

While in my hotel room on a business trip in Hawaii, I became angry to the point of wanting to smash my fist through the wall. I went into the bathroom, shut the door, and put a wet towel on my face. As I stood by the mirror holding the cold towel against my eyes, I heard myself say, **"God, tell me what to do!"**

Instantly, a man's voice spoke to me from my right side: **"Go to church!"**

I jerked my head to the right so fast my neck snapped in two places. There was no one there! I stood alone in an **unusual, absolute silence.**

The voice surprised me, but the empty room shocked me even more. I grabbed the shower curtain and looked behind it–empty! Then I opened the door and hurried out to the bedroom, looked in the closet and under the bed—no one was hiding anywhere! The door was locked and chained! The windows were closed and there was no balcony!

I sat down to think about what had happened. My call to God was like someone else using my voice. I would not have thought to ask God for help. And now, the answer that I had received did not seem to have anything to do with my problem. I could not understand how going to church would help me. But I suddenly realized one thing, **my anger and frustration were gone.**

On Sunday morning, three days later, I asked the hotel desk clerk for directions to the nearest church and walked to the service. This was the first time I had been inside a church in a long time.

After returning to Florida, I cautiously told a few friends about the voice. Some appeared to go rigid, and others acted uncomfortable, as though they did not want to listen, so I stopped talking about it.

"In the day when I cried out, You answered me..." (Psalm 138:3).

"...it is not you who speak, but the Spirit of your Father who speaks in you" (Matthew 10:20).

"...I heard behind me a loud voice... Then I turned to see the voice that spoke with me" (Revelation 1:10, 12).

CHAPTER
2

Strange Advice

Two years after visiting Hawaii, I went to North Carolina for a vacation. A week long dedication program was scheduled at a new church building nearby, and I reluctantly accepted an invitation to attend the opening services. Someone told me a speaker from Orlando, Florida, was having a seminar in the afternoon, and I attended out of curiosity since I lived in Orlando.

He spoke about the Bible for almost an hour. I did not understand much of what he said, because I had rebelled against going to church as a child, and knew nothing about the Bible. He had just finished, and people were standing up and leaving the room, when he asked them to wait. Then he moved to a place where he could look between the people who were standing, fixed his eyes on me, and said, "If there is anyone here from Orlando who is not going to church now, and when they get home they want to go to a good church, I suggest they go to Calvary Assembly." He then told everyone they could leave. While he was right about me being from Orlando and not going to church, I laughed at his suggestion for none of my plans included going to any church.

I did not realize it then, but this was the second time in two years that God told me to go to church.

"...holy men of God spoke as they were moved by the Holy Spirit" (2 Peter 1:21).

CHAPTER
3

Heat Treatment

At the Tuesday evening church service, I was standing with other people while they were singing. I hoped no one would notice that I did not know the words of the songs.

Suddenly, my feet were very hot, and the heat began to flow up my legs. I almost looked down to see if I was standing on a bed of hot charcoal. The heat continued to move up my body all the way to the top of my head. My whole body was so hot I started to perspire.

Then the heat was gone! It had risen slowly, like a thermometer, then disappeared in an instant.

After it left, my eyesight and hearing seemed better, my shoulders were relaxed, and my neck tension was gone. I had an overall sense of well-being, peace and contentment.

No one has ever fully explained my "heat treatment," but I do know God gave me His peace.

"For everyone will be seasoned with fire" (Mark 9:49).

"...and the peace of God, which surpasses all understanding, will guard your hearts and minds..." (Philippians 4:7).

CHAPTER
4

Miracle Baby

The first night of a week of special services, I attended what was called a "Healing Service." During the evening, people claimed to be healed of various health problems. I had never seen anything like this and went back each night to watch what happened. I looked closely for wires, radios, signals, acting or faking, but did not observe anything unusual. Here I was in church, people were singing hymns, and the speaker was teaching from the Bible, but it never occurred to me that God might be healing these people.

Wednesday evening, I was standing in a good viewing spot on the aisle of the fourth row back from the front platform when someone bumped my left shoulder. Turning to my left, I saw a woman walking slowly toward the platform carrying a tiny baby on her right shoulder. Her cheeks and blouse were wet with tears because that small baby, dressed in only a diaper, had two crossed eyes. I thought: **"No wonder she is crying; that poor little baby will have to have operations on both eyes!"** She walked about 10 feet to the edge of the platform and held the baby up to the minister so he could see its face. **"Oh,"** he said gently, **"The little baby has crossed eyes."** He put his hand over the child's grapefruit-size head, prayed for about five seconds, and removed his hand. Then I saw the impossible! Both eyes were straight!

"Stunned" cannot fully describe my reaction. The woman turned and walked past me a second time, less than a minute after she first bumped my shoulder. Once again, I looked at those two small eyes only 18 inches away. **But this time they were perfectly centered!**

Then I lost it. I had seen both eyes, before and after they were healed, and knew **a baby could not pretend to have crossed eyes.** My body trembled and tears streamed down my face as fear of the unknown gripped me. I was on the verge of rushing out of the church when a man's voice spoke to me, calling me by my last name. The voice sounded like it was coming through an invisible earplug connected to a radio and the speaker was talking directly to me!

The voice said: **"Blood, if you believe that healing, and you do, you have got to believe every healing you have seen here this week, and you have got to** believe that God is healing these people, and you have got to believe that God is using John Wesley Fletcher as His instrument to heal these people, and God would not be using John Wesley Fletcher unless he was doing everything God wanted him to do, and all he has been doing is preaching the Bible."

Then suddenly I was deaf! I saw people's lips moving and musical instruments being played but my ears heard nothing. In that silence I heard the voice again: **"Everything in the Bible is true."**

Then my hearing returned and my fear was gone. I stood amazed as I realized God had spoken to me, and I wanted to grab the man next to me and tell him that everything in the Bible is true.

These miracles happened in about one minute, but in that short time my life was changed forever. An awesomeness engulfed me as I finally believed...no... **I more than believed...I knew God was real!** God led me here to see that baby healed so that I would **know** how very real He is—and that is **more than believing!**

"...look with your eyes and hear with your ears, and fix your mind on everything I show you; for you were brought here so that I might show them to you..." (Ezekiel 40:4).

" 'O woman, great is your faith! Let it be to you as you desire.' And her daughter was healed from that very hour" (Matthew 15:28).

"...they were all amazed...and were filled with fear..." (Luke 5:26).

"Will you not tremble at My presence…?" (Jeremiah 5:22).

"…I know you by name" (Exodus 33:17).

"Unless you people see signs and wonders, you will by no means believe" (John 4:48).

CHAPTER
5

Good News

Friday evening, the speaker pointed to me and asked me to come to the platform. I made my way forward wondering why he wanted to talk to me in front of all of these people.

Then he said, **"I have a message for you from God. God wants me to tell you that at one time in your life there was a question in your mind as to whether or not you believed. God wants me to tell you tonight, as you stand here in front of me, that you do believe. Am I telling you the truth?"**

"Yes sir, you are," I replied.

He did not know that the question of whether or not I believed had been a problem for me several years earlier. I met a minister at a motel in South Florida, and we talked for more than three hours about God and Jesus and salvation.

Our conversation was easy and friendly after discovering we were both veterans of the Korean War. He was concerned about my relationship with God, but I would not agree to pray for salvation. I knew there had to be a God, but I did not understand what I was supposed to "believe" or why Jesus dying on a cross would have any effect on me.

Finally, he told me God would accept me just as I was. There was no requirement to attend a church, know anything about the Bible, or perform any service. All that was needed was my willingness to ask God to forgive me and to give Him a chance to work in my life. He also suggested I not reject God when there was an opportunity to accept Him. That was a reasonable offer, and I could not think of any excuse to refuse.

That evening, I walked to the front of a church to accept God and started to think it was a foolish thing to do. I was the first of a few people to reach the platform. Turning to face the congregation, I wished I were somewhere else. I looked at a nearby exit door and thought of walking out, but did not want to break my promise to the minister. I repeated a prayer with the group and could not remember what was said while driving home. The following week, I was baptized in a tank of water but within a month stopped attending church.

I had made the right choice without understanding why. This had been the beginning, a crossroads experience that would not be recognized until four years later when a man in North Carolina, who did not know me, told me, **"You do believe."**

"...the Lord said to him, 'There he is, the man of whom I spoke to you'" (1 Samuel 9:17).

"...whatever the Lord says to me, that I will speak" (1 Kings 22:14).

"I know that you do believe" (Acts 26:27).

"...the natural man does not receive the things of the Spirit of God, for they are foolishness to him..." (1 Corinthians 2:14).

CHAPTER
6

More Good News

My vacation in North Carolina ended and I returned home to Florida. For several days, while I was driving to work, a man's voice spoke in my head with words repeated again and again like a cracked phonograph record: **"You are going to go to Heaven when you die. You are going to go to Heaven when you die."**

While driving home those evenings, I heard the same voice telling me over and over: **"I have a plan for your life. I have a plan for your life."**

This was wild! All I knew about God was what I had seen and heard the week before, and I did not understand much of that. I knew very little about Jesus, almost nothing about the Holy Spirit, and even less about the Bible. Four years ago I had said a prayer without understanding what it meant. But last

Friday, God told me **"You do believe,"** and now He was telling me that I would go to Heaven when I die. **Wow!**

"...whoever believes in Him should not perish but have everlasting life" (John 3:16).

"...we have a building from God, a house not made with hands, eternal in the heavens" (2 Corinthians 5:1).

"For I know the thoughts that I think toward you, says the Lord, thoughts of peace and not of evil, to give you a future and a hope" (Jeremiah 29:11).

How About You?

Do you want to go to Heaven?

Do you want God in your life?

All you have to do is ask Him!

Say this prayer or think it in your head.

God knows your thoughts and will hear you.

"Dear Lord, in the Name of Jesus Christ, Your Son, I ask You to forgive me for everything I have done that hurt You or anyone else. Please fill me with the Holy Spirit and take charge of my life. Thank You, Lord."

CHAPTER
7

Slow Learner

There was another miracle in North Carolina. At one of the first meetings, the speaker asked for $100 donations. I always resented being asked to give money to a church, so this made me angry. Then a guest speaker stood up and spoke for about five minutes.

I did not understand what he said because he spoke about what was written in the Bible. After he finished, I calmly wrote a $100 check. When putting the check in the offering box, I lost all my resentment about giving money to a church and felt good about it. What a miracle that was, for I do not remember anything the speaker said.

Five years later, I was speaking at a breakfast in Florida. I explained the many miracles that happened to me and how my life had changed. However, I did not mention the $100 check. Later that day, I heard a man's voice in my head: **"Why didn't you tell them about the $100? Don't you realize that all of those blessings came upon you after you opened your wallet to God?"**

I am grateful God can change people in an instant and has patience with slow learners.

"I will give you a new heart and put a new spirit within you..." (Ezekiel 36:26).

"And all these blessings shall come upon you and overtake you, because you obey the voice of the Lord your God" (Deuteronomy 28:2).

CHAPTER
8

No Turning Back

Several weeks after seeing the cross-eyed baby, I told some friends about the healing and about God speaking to me. We were sitting in a hotel lounge and it became obvious that they did not want to hear about the miracles. While I was talking, one of the men slammed his fist on the table and said, "Don't give me any of that crap!" Then this highly educated business executive stood up and angrily walked away. I continued talking as two more men left quietly and another one waited patiently for me to finish before leaving me alone at the table.

This was my first experience with negative reactions from people who did not believe or want to hear how real God is. I was not prepared for this from friends, but the rejection did not bother me because I knew what had happened to me was true. It was impossible for me not to know God is real after seeing miracles and hearing His voice. I knew very little about God and nothing about the Bible, but there was no turning back for me. I was committed to learning more about Him in every way possible regardless of what anyone might think.

The following month, the friend who had angrily walked away from the table invited me to lunch and asked me to tell him again what had happened. After hearing the complete story, he became more convinced that God is real, and talked about problems in his life since he had drifted away from church. Then he said he would be returning to church for God's help.

"Go home to your friends, and tell them what great things the Lord has done for you" (Mark 5:19).

"...they have not rejected you, but they have rejected Me..." (1 Samuel 8:7).

"The fear of the Lord is the beginning of wisdom..." (Proverbs 9:10).

PART
2

Miracles Continue

"...I will...show you great and mighty things, which you do not know."

(Jeremiah 33:3)

CHAPTER
9

Empty Bottles

There was a time when I was known to be a heavy drinker. This ended five months after visiting North Carolina.

During a business lunch at a private club, the waitress moved around the table taking our cocktail orders. She talked to a friend next to me while I considered a margarita or a manhattan. Suddenly I heard the words, **"If you really want to stop drinking, you can stop today."**

The voice in my head shocked me and I sat wide-eyed and open-mouthed as the waitress asked for my order. I knew God was giving me an opportunity to change my life if I was willing to do it.

Looking up at her, I heard myself answer, "An iced

tea, please." Every man at that table stopped talking and looked at me in disbelief. Then they glanced at each other, shrugged their shoulders, and resumed their conversations.

That evening I gathered up all the bottles of booze in my home with intentions of giving them to a friend. Then I thought, **if God wanted me to stop, it would not be wise to encourage someone else to drink.** So I opened them and poured the contents down the kitchen drain. I was laughing while thinking what the garbage men would say when so many empty bottles clanked into their truck.

I knew my drinking days were over! In the following weeks, there was no withdrawal, no need to chew gum, nor any other problem or side effect. **Any desire to drink was gone!**

"...choose for yourselves this day whom you will serve..." (Joshua 24:15).

"...they think it strange that you do not run with them in the same flood of dissipation..." (1 Peter 4:4).

CHAPTER
10

Wake-up Call

I was involved in an extended legal situation and decided to ask my attorney to finish the case. At four o'clock the next morning, a loud voice filled my bedroom: **"Be patient, and wait on the Lord!"**

I bolted straight up in bed to a sitting position. While hearing the words clearly, I was startled by being awakened from a sound sleep.

Fearfully, I answered, "Wait! Wait! Is that You Lord? If it is, tell me again! Tell me again so I won't make a mistake!"

The same voice spoke again: **"Be patient, and wait on the Lord!"**

I answered, "OK! OK! I will call my lawyer and have

him tear up the papers. Is that what You want me to do?" As I asked that question, my excitement turned to a calm peace and I knew it was what God wanted. The light on the face of my clock showed exactly four o'clock. Five hours later, I told my attorney to withdraw the case.

This was the second time God had spoken to me by His audible voice. But it would be four years before I fully realized the wisdom of being obedient to this Monday morning wake-up call.

"Whatever I tell you in the dark, speak in the light" (Matthew 10:27).

"...the following night the Lord stood by him and said..." (Acts 23:11).

"...wait for the Lord, and He will save you" (Proverbs 20:22).

"Now the word of the Lord came to Jonah the second time..."(Jonah 3:1).

"...Whatever He says to you, do it" (John 2:5).

CHAPTER
11

Octopus Hand

My right wrist developed a large bump under the skin which was very painful. A doctor told me it was a ganglion cyst and said it was like an octopus, the large bump its head and its tentacles growing up the bone of my arm and along finger bones in my hand. It was not cancerous, but I would have to have an operation on the arm and hand to remove the "tentacles." He told me to take aspirin for the pain until I decided to go to the hospital.

Several weeks of pain and many aspirins later, I was listening to a tape recording of a church service that had taken place the month before. The speaker told everyone who had a health problem to put their hand on the part of their body that needed to be healed. I put my left hand over my right wrist and closed my eyes. The speaker prayed for God's healing and I lifted my left hand. **I looked at my right wrist in amazement! The lump was gone!**

I poked and punched where the bump had been—no pain! I moved, turned, pulled, did everything with the hand, but there was no pain. I was excited and grateful!

For the next 10 days, I could feel the muscles under the skin of my arm and hand moving back over the bones. Every day I felt the space where the tentacles had been become smaller. This was a marvelous confirmation of what the doctor had explained.

"And behold, there was a man who had a withered hand...Then He said to the man, 'Stretch out your hand.' And he stretched it out, and it was restored as whole as the other" (Matthew 12:10,13).

"For I am the Lord who heals you" (Exodus 15:26).

CHAPTER
12

Careful Nurse

Following a businessmen's dinner, I asked a friend to pray for my lower back which had been painful for several days.

He asked me to sit down on a chair and lift my feet off the floor. Then he held my feet under the back of both heels and began to pray. I felt something strange in my hip and leg and sat wide-eyed as **my left leg grew longer and the shoe moved slowly past my right shoe.** After the movement stopped, I stood up and was totally free of pain or discomfort.

Two days later, I was scheduled for an annual physical in a medical clinic. As I stood barefoot under the height measuring device, the nurse called out "6 feet, 3 and 1/2 inches." Then she measured me again and with a frown on her face said, "You have been 6 feet,

3 inches all the years you have been examined here, but now you are 6 feet, 3 and 1/2 inches. The doctor would think I was crazy if I wrote that down, so I am marking you 6 feet, 3 and 1/4 inches."

"...Lord, heal me, for my bones are troubled" (Psalm 6:2).

CHAPTER
13

Rushing Wind

A minister was praying at the end of a church
service in Orlando as I stood with my head bowed.

I was startled by the sound of a hurricane wind.
It lasted only a few seconds and there was not
any feeling of air moving. I raised my head to see
what had happened and, being a tall person,
looked over the sea of bowed heads. None of
them moved so I did not know if anyone else
heard the wind.

The sound was real because it was louder in my
good ear than in the ear damaged in Army service.
Then I thought **"Wow, that is just like the
disciples hearing the Holy Spirit as the sound of
a wind blowing."**

"And suddenly there came a sound from heaven, as of a rushing mighty wind, and it filled the whole house where they were sitting" (Acts 2:2).

CHAPTER
14

Free Fall

I was carrying a box up the inclined metal ramp of a rental truck and struck my head on the edge of the roof. The impact stopped me and I fell backward. While falling through the air, **I could see over my shoulder where my body was going to hit the edge of the ramp** and be broken like a board striking a carpenter's sawhorse.

Suddenly, everything went black—absolute darkness and stillness. I could not see, hear, or feel anything. I thought, "This is strange, I am unconscious but I do not feel any pain from hitting the ramp!" The blackness went away quickly, and **I was inside the back of the truck on my knees with the box still in my arms. I knew God had supernaturally moved me from outside the truck to inside the**

truck, and I said "Thank You, Jesus" over and over again in an overwhelming feeling of gratitude.

The pain in my head from striking the roof was so bad that I grabbed my hair with both hands while tears ran down my cheeks. I began to pray and the **pain went away!** I touched the top of my head and felt a large bump that was tender when touched but otherwise felt like a "hat." There was not any cut, headache, nor other symptom of hitting my head.

I stood up and was amazed at where I was standing. If I had moved there by my own actions, I would have had to climb over and around boxes while carrying a box about two feet square. There was no way I could have done that without knowing it, particularly since my last memory was of falling through the air.

Then I thought that someone may have seen me falling and being moved back into the truck! I hurriedly worked my way around boxes to look out the back of the truck, which was in a parking lot surrounded by apartment buildings. But there was no one—not on any walkway or balcony, or in the parking lot. There were a few birds singing but nothing else, except an **unusual, absolute stillness.**

That night I looked in the Bible to find the people who had been moved from one place to another by the Spirit and was surprised how many there were. The bump remained on my head for almost three months as a reminder of God's miracle.

Then the Spirit entered me and set me on my feet... (Ezekiel 3:24).

"...the Spirit of the Lord caught Philip away... Philip was found at Azotus " (Acts 8:39, 40).

CHAPTER
15

Precious Dottie

I had developed a friendship with a businessman who had a weekly Bible study in his home. One evening, he was hospitalized for emergency surgery and died unexpectedly two weeks later. I was one of his many friends who came to the hospital to visit him and help his wife, Dottie, in any way needed.

After his "homegoing" service, several men of the church volunteered to help Dottie complete a housing project her husband had been building, and I was part of this informal group that assisted her. I met Dottie when attending the Bible study and other church affairs, but only knew her casually prior to her husband's hospitalization.

One afternoon, I left my office and was driving to the building site when a man's voice spoke in my head:

"I am giving her to you as your 'much is given.' I have worked many miracles in your life, but you do not think of these miracles every day. Now, every day when you see her, you will think of Me."

The words startled me and I almost drove off the road. I realized God was talking about marriage to Dottie! I had been involved in two marriages and was planning to live a single life, but God had other plans.

A few days later, I called Dottie and told her about the voice. I was not prepared for her response, "Well, I am not surprised." She told me she had seen me in the church lobby, and heard a voice say, **"He's your next husband."**

She immediately said, "I rebuke you, devil, in the Name of Jesus. I am not going to allow you to put such things in my head." But later, as she sat quietly at home, the voice reminded her: **"The Lord reveals the future to His children."**

She humbly apologized to the Lord!

As we were planning to be married, I learned her name **Dorothy** means "gift of God."

"...He will tell you things to come" (John 16:13).

"For everyone to whom much is given, from him much will be required..." (Luke 12:48).

"...a prudent wife is from the Lord" (Proverbs 19:14).

CHAPTER
16

New Words

While driving on the turnpike, I was listening to
a Bible teaching tape. As the tape ended, I started
thanking God for all the wonderful things He had
done in my life. Then I became aware of something
strange. I was not speaking in the English language!
**My words were in a language I had never heard
and did not understand.**

I was speaking in tongues. Many people had prayed
for me to be able to do this for over a year. Now it
happened when I was alone. I was not aware of when
it began, but I was able to start and stop at will.

"And they were all filled with the Holy Spirit and
began to speak with other tongues..." (Acts 2:4).

PART
3

Miracles Teach

"Resist the devil and he will flee from you."

(James 4:7)

CHAPTER
17

Wrong Voice

I was sitting on the floor of a building in Orlando while attending a meeting with college students. The speaker was talking with a group of students on the platform when he turned and spoke to the audience.

"There is someone here who has been wearing glasses from childhood. You do not like wearing glasses, and God is going to heal your eyes so you will never wear glasses again. Your eyes are getting hot right now. Both eyes are beginning to be hot. All you have to do is stand up and your eyes will be healed."

No one stood so he kept repeating what he had said. Then **my eyeballs began to feel warm and peculiar.** Hoping he might be talking about me, I moved my hand on the floor to push myself up and stand. As

I moved, a voice spoke in my head, **"He is not talking about you. You are an old man. This meeting is for young people. You stand up and everyone will laugh at you. You will only make a fool of yourself."** Twice I started to stand up but stopped when the voice told me I was wrong. The speaker stopped talking about the eyes and went back to the group of students. No one had stood up.

Then I realized my mistake. Because of my fears of failure and rejection, I had believed a negative, condemning voice rather than responding to a respected church leader. In one way that voice had been correct. I did make a fool of myself—by believing the wrong voice. That evening, I asked God to forgive me.

Worst of all, **I had failed God** by not standing to receive His healing. Many young college students would have seen a miracle that might have changed their lives as the cross-eyed baby had changed mine a year and a half earlier.

This was my introduction to the spiritual battlefield, and the first time I realized I had heard words from a demon. It was a valuable, though expensive, lesson.

I also learned that God may give me only one opportunity to do something, and I must be ready to move on His time schedule.

"The fear of man brings a snare, but whoever trusts in the Lord shall be safe" (Proverbs 29:25).

CHAPTER
18

Finally Forgiven

I was willing to do anything God wanted me to do; so I made an appointment with a minister in the church to ask advice on how to handle problems in my life God's way. He identified unforgiveness as a major cause of my conflicts and told me I was unforgiving of my mother. She had died 20 years earlier and I thought I had forgiven her for everything. He explained my unforgiveness had nothing to do with me but was for how she had treated my father. He went on to say that taking up an offense for someone else was harder to forgive than an offense against myself.

He told me to say, "In Jesus' Name, I forgive my mother for..." and then repeat what she had said to my father. I started the prayer and **something supernatural came over me.** My upper body felt scratchy like I was wearing a wool sweater, a choking sensation made breathing and swallowing difficult, and my tongue seemed so thick I could not pronounce words. I stammered through "Je-e-su-us N-a-a-me" and the minister encouraged me to complete the prayer as he and a friend continued to pray for me.

At that moment, **I began to hear voices speak in my head.** One voice was calm and gentle and encouraged me to continue the prayer. Sometimes this voice would precede or follow the minister's guidance using almost the same words. The other voice was demanding in a superior attitude while trying to convince me the prayer was not necessary and would not work. The second voice was very similar to the one I listened to a year earlier when the speaker said someone's eyes would be healed. This time I ignored the demon, and by carefully breathing and controlling my speech, I was able to stammer out the prayer in a low voice. The minister told me to do it again, and this time it was louder but still sounded as if I had a problem talking. The third time I was able to speak more forcefully with each syllable increasing in volume and clarity until the final words were loud and clear.

While still speaking the last words, **the itching feeling left my body like a sweater being pulled over my head, the choking stopped, and my speech was normal. There was also a burning heat in the shape of a hot iron between my shoulders** where I had experienced severe back pain for many years. Then I felt a lightness, as if I had lost weight and recognized a new joy and happiness. **The demon was gone and my back was healed.**

For 26 years, my mother's treatment of my father had been remembered as an unfortunate incident; but I never recognized my own unforgiveness or bitterness. In the following days, I realized a new appreciation and acceptance of women. This proved to be a life-changing event by improving my relationships with both women and men.

"He who passes by and meddles in a quarrel not his own is like one who takes a dog by the ears" (Proverbs 26:17).

"...what is that to you? You follow Me" (John 21:22).

"...if you have anything against anyone, forgive him" (Mark 11:25).

"...you are loosed from your infirmity" (Luke 13:12).

CHAPTER
19

Fast Trip

I was home alone when a man's voice in my head spoke three consecutive phrases with decreasing loudness: **"Seven day fast. Seven day fast. Seven day fast."**

I had never attempted a seven day fast and selected a week with a Friday holiday to insure being home for the last three days.

While standing in my bedroom the afternoon of the sixth day, **I suddenly felt as if the roots of a small tree had been jerked out of my stomach.**

Something demonic had left me! I felt better emotionally and physically and was glad it was gone—whatever it was.

"Is this not the fast that I have chosen: to loose the bonds of wickedness...?" (Isaiah 58:6).

"This was done three times..." (Acts 10:16).

CHAPTER
20

Night Attack

I awoke suddenly from a sound sleep and realized **I could not move. It seemed as if air pressure or a supernatural force was pushing my body down flat on the bed**. I could blink my eyes but not move any other part of my body. My heart was beating rapidly, I felt wet from perspiration, and it was difficult to breathe. Then there was pain on the left side of my chest like a concrete building block sitting on my ribs.

There was no reason for these things although the weight and pain on my chest made me think of a heart attack. Then I realized the pain on my left side was not inside my body, but on the outside, under the "weight." I forced myself to breathe slowly then spoke with difficulty, "Jesus." I repeated, this time with a stronger voice. "Jesus." Finally, as I spoke "Jesus" with all possible force, **every feeling of pain, weight and pressure left me.**

Grateful and relieved, I lay on the bed for a few moments before realizing my pajamas were wet with perspiration. I got up, dried off with a towel, put on dry pajamas, changed the sheets, and went back to bed.

God gave me His peace and I was not fearful of anything during this oppression. I was grateful for His peace because fear could have caused me to cry out to people for help, and this might have caused me to have a heart attack.

"...he cried out, saying 'Lord, save me!' " (Matthew 14:30).

"Death and life are in the power of the tongue..." (Proverbs 18:21).

"...just as you have spoken in My hearing, so I will do to you" (Numbers 14:28).

CHAPTER
21

Honey Jar

I was in the kitchen making a peanut butter and honey sandwich. Without warning, the metal spoon I was holding in the honey jar started clanging against the glass as my hand shook uncontrollably. At the same time, the rest of **my body began shaking.** I was hot with fever, my stomach felt as if I were going to throw up, my head ached, and dizziness and weakness began to take effect. In an instant, I felt all the symptoms of the flu.

I began to rebuke each symptom. **"Fever, I rebuke you in the Name of Jesus; headache, I rebuke you in the Name of Jesus; stomach-ache, I rebuke you in the Name of Jesus; shaking, I rebuke you in the Name of Jesus; dizziness, I rebuke you in the Name of Jesus; weakness, I rebuke you in the Name of Jesus."**

My body was shaking so much, it was difficult to speak the first words. As I repeated the rebukes, my voice became stronger and the words more pronounced.

Then it ended, as quickly as it started. All symptoms were gone and my hand firmly held the spoon in the honey jar.

"So He...rebuked the fever, and it left her" (Luke 4:39).

"Then He arose and rebuked the wind... And the wind ceased..." (Mark 4:39).

CHAPTER
22

Laughing Boxer

While sitting on the edge of my bed, I felt light blows on my legs, body and arms. I moved my hands to stop what seemed to be invisible little people hitting me with boxing gloves. The blows did not hurt, but would not stop.

As each blow hit my body, I swung my hand in that direction. After several seconds, **I began to chuckle.** The thought of swinging at demons I could not see was funny. I stopped moving and started laughing. With the laughter, the blows slowed and then stopped.

Laughter is also a weapon to defeat demons.

"Is this the man who made the earth tremble…?" (Isaiah 14:16)

"You shall laugh at destruction..." (Job 5:22).

CHAPTER
23

Wood Carvings

During a business trip in South America, I had purchased a small wood carving of a stone statue on Easter Island in the Pacific Ocean. On a visit to Canada, I acquired a carved model of a wooden totem pole handcrafted by a North American Indian. Both items were prominently displayed on a table in my office.

As I walked by the table one afternoon, a man's voice spoke in my head: **"Idols!"**

I said, "Idols?"

The voice spoke again: **"Idols!"**

Then I understood. Anything that people worshiped as another god is an offense to the true God. I took the wooden carvings down the hall, smashed them, and threw them in the trash container. Soon afterwards, I started to "clean house" of all souvenirs, gifts, books, whatever related to ancient or modern religions, witchcraft, horoscopes, fortune telling and anything that conflicted with the Bible.

"...every man shall throw away his idols..." (Isaiah 31:7).

"You shall have no other gods before Me" (Exodus 20:3).

"You shall not make mention of the name of their gods"...(Joshua 23:7).

CHAPTER
24

Wrong Club

I was a member of the Masons and had continued to pay dues although I was inactive.

A friend noticed my Masonic ring and gave me a pamphlet which claimed the organization did not follow Biblical principles. I questioned that since God was referred to in meetings. Some rituals also appeared to follow events in the Bible, and members received a personalized Bible after joining. However, the rituals were secret and personal oaths required promises that rejected Bible teachings. The Name "Jesus" was never mentioned and some people were denied membership by a secret voting procedure.

After further investigation, it was clear to me that the pamphlet was right. I renounced the oaths I had taken, resigned my membership, and asked God to forgive me for having been a member of the Masons. Then I threw out my ring and anything related to the organization. A week later I was at my desk in the bedroom and felt impressed that something else was in the house. Looking around the room, I remembered what had been overlooked. Moving to my dresser and opening a drawer, I removed a large envelope from under some clothing. Inside was the lambskin apron given me after completing one of the membership requirements.

I said, "I am going to throw this in the trash!" **Instantly, I heard a "pop" like a small firecracker and felt something leave my body!** I quickly went outside and threw the envelope into the trash can!

There was a demonic bondage connected with that organization. I later learned that many Masonic symbols can be traced back hundreds of years to Egyptian worship of idols and pagan ceremonies.

"For it is shameful even to speak of those things which are done by them in secret" (Ephesians 5:12).

"...they commanded that they should not speak in the Name of Jesus" (Acts 5:40).

"But we have renounced the hidden things of shame..." (2 Corinthians 4:2).

"If we confess our sins, He is faithful and just to forgive us" (1 John 1:9).

PART
4

Miracles Change

**"...learn from Me....and you will find rest for
your souls."**

(Matthew 11:29)

CHAPTER
25

Big Mistake

A warehouse tenant came to my office to pay his rent and told me of the success of his new business, which he considered to be the result of his good planning and hard work.

After he finished talking, I told him about many of the miracles and the reality of God in my life. Then I offered to help him invite God into his life. He had been very interested while listening to me so I was surprised when he said, "No." He told me he had been living with his parents since graduating from college and was attending church with them. The business was growing, he had money and friends, and was happy with things just as they were. Then he said, **"I do not need God."**

When I heard the words, "I do not need God," I felt

pain in my stomach as if someone had kicked me, and my body seemed to shudder. I talked with him for several more minutes, but he was strong in his decision to reject God. I knew he was making a big mistake, and I was fearful for him while thinking to myself **"Oh, I wish he had not said that!"**

Less than three months later, the young man's mother called me and asked if he could cancel his lease contract. He was not able to work after being stricken with leukemia, and he had almost died several weeks earlier.

I believe this is an example of what can happen when a person thinks they can get along without God.

"Do not be deceived. God is not mocked…" (Galatians 6:7).

"And do not grieve the Holy Spirit of God…" (Ephesians 4:30).

"…He might humble you and…test you, to do you good in the end" (Deuteronomy 8:16).

"The Lord…is longsuffering toward us, not willing that any should perish…" (2 Peter 3:9).

CHAPTER
26

No More Worry

For several years, my life continued to be complicated with family conflicts, stress in my job and financial problems. I knew the answers to my problems were in the Bible but did not know where to find them. Fortunately, I was reading a Bible that had footnotes to explain important subjects, and I read it in the morning, during lunch and every evening. When reading about the blessings from God, I would ask for them, then feel rejected when they did not happen. Even though I prayed for things to get better, they got worse, and I cried out, "Why me, Lord?" After learning all things are possible for God, but seeing my situations did not change, I asked Him, "What is going on?" **But I knew God is real and never gave up hope that He would help me**.

One morning I was so upset that I did not want to go to work. As I sat on the edge of my bed, a man's voice spoke in my head**: "Trust and obey. Trust and obey. Trust and obey."**

These three statements started out loud, then lower, and finally a whisper. As the last phrase ended, the oppression lifted.

Things went well for several days until the oppression returned. Then the voice spoke again in the same tones as before, and I had a feeling of being revived: **"All things are possible, only believe. All things are possible, only believe. All things are possible, only believe."**

Then I began to understand how verses in the Bible could help me. Abraham was willing and obedient to give his son to God and was told he would be blessed (see Genesis 22:12-18). Samuel was given to God by his parents when he was a child, and God made Samuel a great leader of his country (1 Samuel 1:11, 28; 3:19-20). Jesus told Peter that what happened to John was none of his business. All Peter had to do was follow Jesus (John 21:22-23).

These convinced me that if I would trust and obey God and release my family, job, money, and everything to Him, He would help me and He would take care of the people and things I gave to Him.

After years of worry, it was not easy to stop. When I began to be concerned about a problem, I stopped, spoke to God, and turned it over to Him again. As

I continued to do this and trust God more, my anxieties decreased. I also noticed many problems were being resolved without my worrying.

For a short time I even felt guilty about not worrying. But if God cannot handle all my problems, nobody can. I am very happy to turn them over into His care.

"...do not worry..." (Matthew 6:25-34).

"...for with God all things are possible" (Mark 10:27).

"...do not turn aside from following the Lord..." (1 Samuel 12:20).

"Come to Me...and I will give you rest" (Matthew 11:28).

"Trust in the Lord with all your heart, and lean not on your own understanding" (Proverbs 3:5).

"Casting all your care upon Him, for He cares for you" (1 Peter 5:7).

CHAPTER
27

Depression Cure

Even though my life was changing, depression was an unwanted companion for months. It grew out of guilt for many things I had done or failed to do. Although my parents died many years ago, I felt great sorrow for failing to establish a closer relationship with them. It was worse with my own family. I had inflicted emotional pain on my wives, and my selfishness had caused me to be less of a father than I now realized I should have been. I had hurt many people and the desire to change the past was overwhelming.

The only way to rebuild my life was to put God first and keep Him at the center of everything. I started by asking Him to forgive me for the things I had done wrong and for the pain I had caused people. After admitting the things I could remember, I asked God to remind me of those I had forgotten. As

He brought them to my mind, I confessed them.
When I remembered my experiences as a youth and
young man, I became aware of more people who were
hurt by my rebellion and self-centered actions. I recalled
broken promises, unfaithful acts, things said and done
because of pride or stubbornness, lies going back to
my childhood, bad reactions in times of fear or anger,
damage caused in ignorance and much more. It was
a humbling experience which I never regretted.
I felt a freedom from guilt with each confession that
was like a heavy pack being removed from my back.

Following my confessions to God, **I forgave people
for things they had done to hurt or disappoint me.**
This started with my parents and included many who
had died and others whose names I did not remember.
It was hard to forgive some people. Sometimes I wanted
to punish them but knew that was up to God. Finally,
I asked God to help me have unconditional forgiveness
for them day after day until I really believed what I was
saying. I was then able to forgive everyone just as God
had forgiven me. The disappointment, anger, frustration,
knots in my stomach, desire to get even and bad
reactions to memories were gone. I even found
pleasure in praying for them afterwards.

After forgiving other people, **I forgave God for what
I had wrongfully blamed on Him.** Now that I knew
Him as my Creator, I felt foolish for questioning what
He did or allowed to happen to me or other people.
Many of these experiences made me more grateful to

God. They were testimonies of how He will forgive
and change me. Now, most of all, I wanted to do
things His way and not mine. I realized it is better to
let Him take charge of my life and not complain about
what happens to me or anyone else.

Finally, **I tried to forgive myself.** This was the most
difficult after understanding how deeply I had hurt some
people. As I struggled with guilt and condemnation, a
man's voice spoke in my head: **"Rich young ruler."**

I quickly searched for this Bible story and found it in
Mark 10, verse 17. A man asked Jesus what to do in
order to have eternal life. After answering his questions,
Jesus **"loved him"** and said, **"Follow Me."** The man
did not do what Jesus suggested and walked away.
Suddenly, I understood another meaning to the story.
The man made a fully informed, free will choice not to
do what Jesus told him, and no one stopped him. Jesus
had the ability to change the man's mind as He did
mine, but He did nothing. Jesus could have called the
man back or sent someone after him to talk to him,
but although He loved him, He did nothing.

God showed me through this Bible story that He will
let people make choices even when they make a
wrong choice. I am responsible for my own thoughts
and actions, and have freedom to choose the right or
wrong way to do everything. **I cannot blame my
problems on my parents or anyone else,** or use
what they did or did not do for me as an excuse.

While I am accountable to God for what I think and do, **I am not accountable to God for the choices of other people,** even if they blame me for problems in their life.

A few days later, the voice spoke in my head again: **"Who are you not to forgive yourself, seeing I have forgiven you?"**

That did it. The depression left after I understood that **forgiveness is a miracle from God** which allows me to be free from guilt and condemnation after He has forgiven me. However, freedom from guilt and condemnation does not mean I can ignore my wrong actions. **I asked people to forgive me and made restitution to correct past mistakes when possible.**

These experiences also showed me how to live a **"forgiving life."** When I think or do anything that would not please God, I quickly ask Him to forgive me and do not feel guilty for what I did. When people upset me in any way, I forgive them just as God has forgiven me, and do not allow their actions to make me angry or bitter. This helps me keep the peace of God which is very important to me.

"Anxiety in the heart of man causes depression..." (Proverbs 12:25).

"Who are you that you should be afraid...?"
(Isaiah 51:12)

"Then you will remember your evil ways and
your deeds that were not good; and you will
loathe yourselves in your own sight..."
(Ezekiel 36:31).

"If we confess our sins, He is faithful and just to
forgive us our sins and to cleanse us..." (1 John 1:9).

"Repent...so that times of refreshing may come..."
(Acts 3:19).

"...and you are clean" (John 13:10).

"... If you have anything against anyone, forgive
him..." (Mark 11:25).

"There is... no condemnation to those who are
in Christ Jesus..." (Romans 8:1).

"And the peace of God...will guard your hearts
and minds..." (Philippians 4:7).

CHAPTER
28

Instruction Manual

When the voice spoke to me in Hawaii, my reaction was "How about that? God spoke to me. That was nice." But when driving home from North Carolina two years later, my thoughts were **"God is real! The Bible is true! Wow!"**

The greatest change in my life began with seeing the baby healed and hearing God's voice. One minute of supernatural understanding had wiped out 52 years of foolish ignorance. I did not love God and did not know He loved me! I was not looking for God and did not know He had **always** been looking for me. I was simply overwhelmed by knowing that **an invisible Spirit with power to do miracles and talk to people, also created the Bible so we can learn about Him.**

For the first time in my life I had a driving ambition,

an all-consuming craving to read the Bible and learn
about God. Nothing else mattered. God was real and
I knew it but I felt like a stranger in a foreign country
and did not know what to do. I started by going to
church, after locating the one suggested by the speaker
at the seminar. Then I found another Bible-teaching
church and went to both of them—three different
services on Sunday and one Wednesday night. My free
time was committed to reading the Bible, which took
10 months the first time to read cover to cover. (Now
I read through it every year and miracles continue to
happen.)

I also learned from Christian radio and TV, church
seminars, Bible studies in a friend's home, and
meetings of a Christian men's group. As time went
on I noticed changes which I called my "lost and
found" experiences:

The **"peace"** that God had given me grew
stronger after losing the fear of death by knowing
I would go to Heaven.

I lost my enjoyment of telling or listening to
vulgar jokes, and stopped cursing without
knowing what was happening.

An **"empty"** feeling inside me was replaced with
a **"fullness."**

I lost my desire for alcohol and did not even
enjoy the smell of booze. After losing my

drinking friends, I found new friendships with people in church.

I lost my compulsion to gamble at poker and other card games.

Money became less important and I lost my desire to have "things."

I sold my guns after my attitude changed about killing game animals and birds.

After being forgiven by God, and forgiving other people and myself, I felt clean and free from guilt, condemnation and shame, and found a new self-respect.

When reading the Bible, I overcame rejection and found real self-confidence while learning about God and how to change my living habits.

I stopped having lustful thoughts about women. Patience and self-control replaced my anger, rebellion, quick temper, and hasty actions.

I found a growing gratitude for how God is changing me, and a desire to tell people what He is doing in my life.

Four years before seeing the baby healed, a minister talked me into saying a prayer when I did not fully understand what I was doing. God honored that prayer because **I was willing to give Him a chance to work on me**. God will also honor you if you invite Him into your life. All you have to do is say a prayer as I did:

"Dear Lord, in the Name of Jesus Christ, Your Son, I ask You to forgive me for everything I have done that hurt You or anyone else. Please fill me with the Holy Spirit and take charge of my life. Thank You, Lord."

Wonderful! You have made the most important choice of your life.

Reading the Bible is the most important thing I do to keep my relationship with God. I read the Bible every day, never doubting anything in it because it is all true. It is the instruction manual for living life. I also understand the Bible because I have received the Holy Spirit, and **"...the Holy Spirit...will teach you all things..."** (John 14:26). God has made this easy by giving me only one Book to read. Everything He wants me to know is in the Holy Bible.

Every day I ask God to teach me and help me understand the Bible. Then I read a Chapter in Proverbs. There are 31 short Chapters, and I read the Chapter that matches the date. On the first day of the month, I read Chapter 1. In a 30 day month, I read Chapters 30 and 31 on the 30th.

Proverbs deals with daily living. When reading

a Proverb **that makes me feel guilty,** I ask God to forgive me for what I did that causes the guilt. The next month I am free of guilt when reading that Proverb. God's Word is true as Psalm 119:6,9 states:

"Then I would not be ashamed, when I look into all Your commandments.... How can a young man cleanse his way? By taking heed according to Your word."

My Bible has 1217 pages. I can read four pages a day and finish the whole Bible in 10 months, but it usually takes me a year. The first time I started in Genesis and read through Revelation. Now I mix them up by reading some in the New Testament and some in the Old Testament: Matthew, then Genesis, then Mark, then Exodus, etc. There are many ways to read the Bible. The important thing is to do it!

I have a Bible that is easy to read. It has the words of Jesus printed in red, and footnotes that explain the main events. When words or verses have a special meaning to me, I mark them with a pencil, ball point pen, crayon, or dry marker. (Wet markers may bleed through the paper.) Bibles are also printed with large letters for easier reading, and have been recorded on tapes for listening. These are available in Bible bookstores listed in the Yellow Pages of most telephone directories.

"...seek first the kingdom of God and His righteousness, and all these things will be added to you" (Matthew 6:33).

"...the Lord says: '...Those who honor Me I will honor...' " (1 Samuel 2:30).

"...He is a rewarder of those who diligently seek Him" (Hebrews 11:6).

CHAPTER
29

Words to Remember

I have memorized the "Lord's Prayer" of Matthew 6:9-13, Psalm 23, and part of Psalm 103. When saying "Our Father in Heaven," I remember how God has changed my life. When saying, "And forgive us our debts," I am grateful He has forgiven me. Many times I feel the presence of the Holy Spirit while speaking the words in these Scriptures.

Lord's Prayer

"Our Father in heaven,
Hallowed be Your Name.
Your kingdom come.
Your will be done
On earth as it is in heaven.
Give us this day our daily bread.

And forgive us our debts,
As we forgive our debtors.
And do not lead us into temptation,
But deliver us from the evil one.
For Yours is the kingdom and the power
and the glory forever.
Amen."

Psalm 23

"The Lord is my shepherd;
I shall not want.
He makes me to lie down in green pastures;
He leads me beside the still waters.
He restores my soul;
He leads me in the paths of righteousness
For His Name's sake.
Yea, though I walk through the valley
of the shadow of death,
I will fear no evil;
For You are with me;
Your rod and Your staff
they comfort me.
You prepare a table before me
in the presence of my enemies;
You anoint my head with oil;
My cup runs over.
Surely goodness and mercy shall follow me
All the days of my life;
And I will dwell in the house of the Lord
Forever."

Psalm 103:1-5

"Bless the Lord, 0 my soul;
And all that is within me, bless His holy Name!
Bless the Lord, 0 my soul,
And forget not all His benefits:
Who forgives all your iniquities,
Who heals all your diseases,
Who redeems your life from destruction,
Who crowns you with lovingkindness and
tender mercies,
Who satisfies your mouth with good things,
So that your youth is renewed like the eagle's."

"All Scripture is given by inspiration of
God...that the man of God may be complete,
thoroughly equipped for every good work"
(2 Timothy 3:16-17).

CHAPTER
30

Nothing New

There is nothing new or unusual about the miracles that happened to me or the changes in my life afterwards.

When I saw the cross-eyed baby, I had **"turned aside"** to see the **"great sight "** of people being healed. While I was watching, God called my name and spoke to me just as He did when Moses stopped to look at the burning bush.

> **"Moses said, 'I will now turn aside and see this great sight, why the bush does not burn.' So when the Lord saw that he turned aside to look, God called to him... 'Moses!'... And Moses...was afraid..."** (Exodus 3:3, 4, 6).

I knew God is real after seeing the cross-eyed baby

healed and hearing His voice. Many other people also believed in God after seeing a miracle on Mount Carmel in Israel.

"Then the fire of the Lord fell and consumed the burnt sacrifice... Now when all the people saw it, they fell on their faces; and they said, 'The Lord, He is God! The Lord, He is God!' "
(1 Kings 18:38, 39).

Five days after I believed God is real, He told me that I was going to go to Heaven when I die. Jesus told a criminal hanging on a cross the same thing, and the man knew very little about God.

"And Jesus said to him, 'Assuredly, I say to you, today you will be with Me in Paradise' "
(Luke 23:43).

Saul of Tarsus holds the record for life changes. Saul was so angry with Jesus that he killed, imprisoned, and threatened people who believed in Him. He was on a trip to Damascus to arrest more people when Jesus appeared and spoke to him along the road. Saul instantly knew he had been wrong about Jesus. He changed his name from Saul to Paul, and as Paul the Apostle, he wrote 13 of the 27 books in the New Testament of the Bible. This angry, stubborn, violent, and heartless man who had murdered, beaten, jailed, and frightened men, women, and children, suddenly became a preacher of Jesus Christ and a teacher of love and compassion. (Acts 9:1-22; 22:3-21; 26:9-20).

Paul the Apostle is proof to me that God can change anyone's life.

I have asked God to bless every person who reads this book, and I know something good is going to happen to you.

"For the promise is to you and to your children" (Acts 2:39).

About the Author

William Carr Blood was born at home in East Rochester, New York, and now resides in Orlando, Florida, with his wife Dorothy.

He lived outside the United States for over nine years, primarily in Germany, France, Korea and Japan. After a 20 year career as an officer in the United States Army, he held positions in intermodal transportation and international business. He attended North Georgia College, graduated from the University of Maryland, is a Certified Member of the American Society of Transportation and Logistics (Emeritus), and a former director of the National Association of Foreign-Trade Zones.

Miracles! has been translated into Chinese and Russian. His second book, *The Final Exodus,* has also been published in Russia.

Additional copies available through your local
Christian Bookstore or:

Lift Jesus Higher Ministry, Inc.
P. O. Box 587
Carrollton, GA 30117
Phone (770) 832-2102
FAX (770) 838-1915
or
Email: miraclesbd@earthlink.net
William Carr Blood
Phone or Fax (407) 876-3793